EXTRAORDINARY!

THE BOOK THAT MAKES YOU FEEL HAPPY

Written by Poppy O'Neill

Illustrated by Caribay M. Benavides

Consultant: Wynne Kinder, MEd

MOVE and DANCE, MAKE STUFF, get CREATIVE, be HAPPY, LEARN about YOURSELF.

WINDMILL BOOKS

A Message from Wynne Kinder, Teacher and mindfulness expert

Hey, Extraordinary Reader!

This book is made for you. It fits you. Because just like you, this book is extraordinary – it is **unique, useful,** and **fun** too!

The Extraordinary Book That Makes You Feel Happy is unique because the way you experience it, and what you create with it, will be unique to you!

It is **useful** because it can inspire you to notice the real you, help you figure out what you need, and guide you to take really good care of yourself.

And **fun** too? You bet! This book is full of so many fun things to **explore, try, do, play, make, create, share,** and **keep!**

Here's how to get started:

- Sit in a comfortable spot, maybe in your favorite place to settle.
- Shift around until you can be comfortable. Pause there for a bit.
- Take a look at the contents and choose where to start:
    - at the beginning?
    - with a word or phrase that matches how you feel?
    - perhaps with a fun idea that catches your eye?
        - Go there and take your time looking, reading, and imagining.

Remember, you can feel happy by noticing, choosing, trying, learning, caring, and exploring your extraordinary self within the pages of this extraordinary book.

Enjoy!

CONTENTS

1

Practice yoga to stretch your body.

MOVE YOUR BODY

to free your emotions

Moving your body helps emotions to move through and out of you. When your body moves, your brain feels good. Let's move!

Take a deep breath in and out. Shake and wiggle your whole body in whichever way feels good.

Pigeon pose

Hold your head up high and breathe deeply.

Butterfly pose

Flutter your knees up and down.

Swan pose

Feel the stretch in your legs.

You are the expert on how your body feels. How does your body want to move right now?

Would it feel good to jump up and down?

Do your arms want to sweep back and forth?

How do your hips want to move?

Follow the yoga poses below when you need a good stretch. Hold each pose for three breaths.

Bear pose

See how straight you can get your legs.

Lizard pose

How low can you go?

Gorilla pose

Feel the stretch behind your knees.

2

Make some delicious, healthy snacks.

TAKE CARE OF YOUR BODY

to take care of your mind

Eating healthily, drinking plenty of water, and getting enough sleep are the building blocks of a happy mind.

When you feel hungry, eat a healthy snack to boost your mind and your body.

Frozen yogurt pops

2 cups yogurt - dairy, coconut, or almond

2 tbsp natural sweetener - honey, maple, or agave syrup

Fresh, soft fruit

1 Mash your fruit into a puree.

2 Mix in the yogurt and sweetener.

3 Pour into ice pop molds and freeze for 4 hours.

4 Your yogurt pops are ready to enjoy!

When it's time to sleep, imagine starlight shining on your toes, relaxing them one by one.

As the light moves up your body, think about relaxing each part of you.

When the starlight reaches the top of your head, you're ready for sleep.

Energy balls

1.5 cups chopped dates

1/2 cup oats

1 tbsp maple syrup

optional extras – cocoa powder, chopped nuts, shredded coconut

1. Soak the dates in hot water for five minutes.
2. Drain the dates and mix all ingredients together.
3. Squish into 1-inch (2.5 cm) balls.
4. Chill in the fridge for at least half an hour.

3

Write about your feelings in a journal.

SPEAK YOUR MIND

because your voice matters

Speaking about your thoughts, feelings, and experiences helps you to understand yourself and lets others get to know the real you.

Sometimes we keep our thoughts and feelings inside, but what's important needs to be let out.

Buy a blank notebook. Write My Journal on the cover and decorate.

Even if a problem can't be solved, talking to someone you trust will help you feel better.

In your journal write the words below on each day of the week to start you off.

Monday

Today I went...

Tuesday

Today I felt...

Wednesday

Today I enjoyed...

Thursday

Today I learned...

Friday

Today I felt...

Saturday

Today I went...

Sunday

Today I learned...

4

Make a starry breathing wand.

TAKE A DEEP BREATH

to relax your mind and body

Imagine breathing in the Solar System.

Taking a big breath wakes you up and gets you ready for anything.

Breathing out is one of the simplest ways to create calm.

Stretch up high and fill with air.

Breathe out slowly and reach down gradually to catch a shooting star.

If you feel anxious, take a finger hike. It will make you feel much calmer. Walk your finger up and down the mountains as you breathe in and out to the count of five.

Make a breathing wand

You will need

cardstock 8 in x 3 in (20cm x 8cm)

tissue paper

tape

scissors

1 Cut out a cardstock strip. Roll into a cylinder and secure with tape.

2 Cut the tissue paper into thin strips and tape the strips inside one edge.

3 Take a big breath in and watch the streamers wave as you breathe out.

5

Chill out with mosaic art.

RESET
to rest and relax

Sometimes you need to reset before you can rest and relax. You can let go of extra energy in lots of different ways.

Try running, jumping, skipping, or Hula-Hooping.

To rest and relax, cut out lots of little squares to make a soothing piece of mosaic art.

You will need

1 Cut out some strips of colored paper.

2 Cut along the strips to make lots of little squares of paper.

3 Glue the squares onto a picture or just make a pattern.

Relax with art

Find an old magazine and cut out lots of little squares in different colors. Trace just the outlines of this picture onto a piece of card or paper. Use the mosaic squares to fill in your picture.

Make mosaic art

Create your own pictures by cutting out, arranging, and gluing the colored squares into pictures or patterns.

6

Be motivated with positive messages.

BE POSITIVE

– believe in yourself and try your best

When you're learning something new, each mistake helps you improve. When you think you can't do something, try adding "yet."

Each time you practice, you make progress.

You can do it!

Just be you.

You are braver than you think!

Try your best.

Keep going!

Reach for the stars.

One step at a time.

Be curious.

When you look for positivity, you'll find it all around you.

Write the positive messages on sticky notes or bits of cardstock and put them where you can see them to help keep you motivated.

Imagine the possibilities!	You've got this.	You can take a break.	You are determined.
You are enough.	You are awesome!	You are kind.	You have courage.

7 CARE FOR YOUR BODY

because it's your forever home

Pick a move to show your body some love.

Your body is incredible in so many ways. When you are kind to your body, you feel good all over.

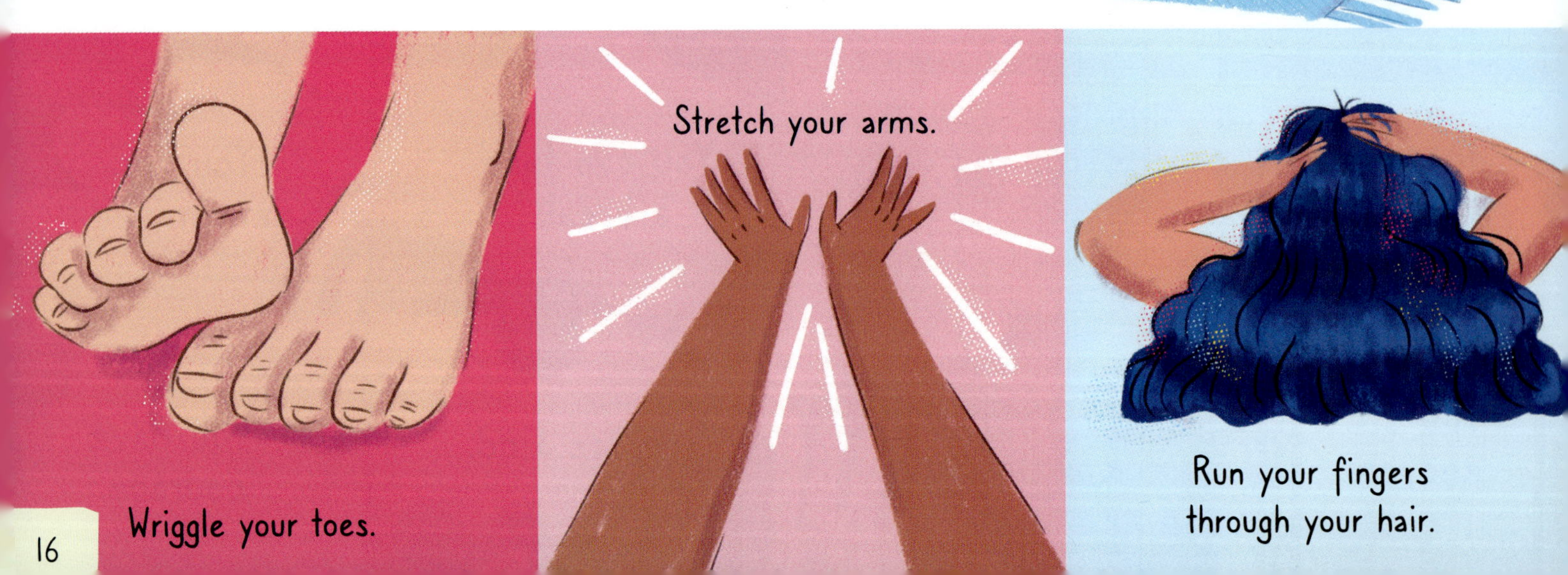

Sit comfortably and say thank you to your body!

Thank you eyes for showing me the world.

Thank you tongue for the delicious tastes.

Thank you legs for helping me to walk and play.

How will you say thank you to your body?

Put your hand on your heart.

Boop your nose.

Stretch your legs.

8

Find calm in your never-ending garden.

GUIDE YOUR THOUGHTS

to calm them

Sometimes thoughts can spin out of control. Learn to guide them by visiting a secret garden in your mind.

Picture a magical garden. What can you see? You can fill it with anything you like.

Look at each picture. Ask yourself what this scene would sound like or smell like. What would would you hear?

Calm your mind

Focus on your finger as you follow the moonlit trail through this garden maze.

9

Send a note to make your friends smile.

BE TRUE TO YOURSELF

because it's wonderful to be you

What do you love to do?

What inspires you?

What makes you different is what makes you special. Your interests are a big part of what makes you unique.

What do you dream about doing?

What do you know lots about?

Cut a square of cardstock or paper. Decorate and write a message to someone who is special to you.

You're special because

From:

You're unique talent is

From:

You make me smile

From:

You're my friend because

From:

10

Color your way to mindfulness.

BE MINDFUL

– take a moment to just "be"

Your senses and imagination can help you practice just being.

Close your eyes and picture the ocean.

As you breathe in, imagine the waves moving forward.

As you breathe out, think about the waves moving away.

Take a deep breath for a really big wave.

Trace or copy these waves onto paper. Color them in. Watch as the color fills the gaps.

Close your eyes and imagine a beautiful forest all around you. In front of you is a pond of still water.

You can see your reflection in the pond. You can see the trees and sky in it too.

Swirl your finger around in the water and watch the ripples it makes.

When the water is still again, open your eyes.

Trace or copy this picture onto paper. Color the pond like the one you imagined.

11

Make and string up some positivity flags.

RESPECT YOURSELF

and be your own best friend

Treat yourself the way you would like be treated. Be kind to yourself and be your own biggest fan.

I WILL STAND UP FOR MYSELF

I WILL BE A GOOD FRIEND

I WILL TRY MY BEST

I WILL BE BRAVE

Each morning, think of one wish for the day.

Say kind words to yourself. The more you say them, the more you will believe they are true.

Cut out some paper or card triangles. Write kind words on them. Make holes at the flat end of each triangle.

Thread your flags on some string and hang them up together.

12

Send some happiness on a postcard.

FIND HAPPINESS

to grow happiness

The more time you spend doing things that bring you happiness, the easier it becomes to look for happiness everywhere you go.

Smiling works like magic. It makes your mind and body feel relaxed and happy.

Sharing happiness helps to grow happiness. Make someone smile by sending them a postcard.

Fill a shelf, box, or drawer with things that make you smile.

Visit your special place whenever you need a boost of happiness.

Cut out rectangles of card-stock to make postcards. Draw a picture on the front or stick on a funny photo. Send a card to someone you care about or leave it somewhere for them to find.

13

Make a face to match your feelings.

NAME YOUR EMOTIONS

to accept them all

Naming your feelings can help you learn what's really going on inside. There's no such thing as a bad or a wrong emotion.

What do you feel today?

Emotions are like colors. The rainbow is not complete without all of them.

Everyone feels a whole rainbow of emotions, even if they don't always show every color!

The emotions you feel are part of what makes you special.

On paper, draw and cut out features like the ones shown here.

Draw some big faces on some cardstock. Stick the features on the faces to make different expressions.

14

Make an expressive, spinning face.

EXPRESS YOURSELF

to let your feelings out

When you let your feelings show, you are being true to you. Your emotions can tell a truthful story.

Which words and pictures could you use to express your feelings?

You will need

Make a spinning face

1. Cut a circle of cardstock 4 in (10cm) in diameter..
2. Draw a face on one side and an upside down face on the other. Change one feature.
3. Punch a hole on the left and right.

Big feelings can be tricky to show on the outside.
Dancing lets you express yourself freely.

Put some music on and dance to put a smile on your face!

4 Thread a rubber band through each hole..

5 Fasten each rubber band by threading it back through itself.

Twist the rubber bands and let the circle spin.

What do you see?

15

Give a thank you card to show you're grateful.

FEEL GRATEFUL
for the little things

Practice looking for things to be grateful for. You'll be able to find joy in the most unexpected places.

Look around you. How many things can you spot that you feel grateful for?

Choose two people to give cards to and write why you are thankful.

Who are you grateful for?

Make and decorate thank you cards. Use these pictures for ideas.

Dear ....

Thank you for

....

....

....

....

from ....

Dear ....

Thank you for

....

....

....

....

from ....

16

Make a scrapbook to celebrate you.

LOVE YOURSELF

because you are unique

You are always with yourself, so make sure you are a good friend to you.

Care for yourself by giving yourself a big hug.

Make a self-love scrapbook all about you. You can draw on the pages, or stick things on with glue.

Find your anchor

Emotions are like the sea, always moving and changing. Create an anchor of positive thoughts to steady you, however many waves might come.

Thinking and saying positive words to yourself helps you feel calm and be kind to yourself no matter what is happening.

My three wishes

1
2
3

....

....

My best hug

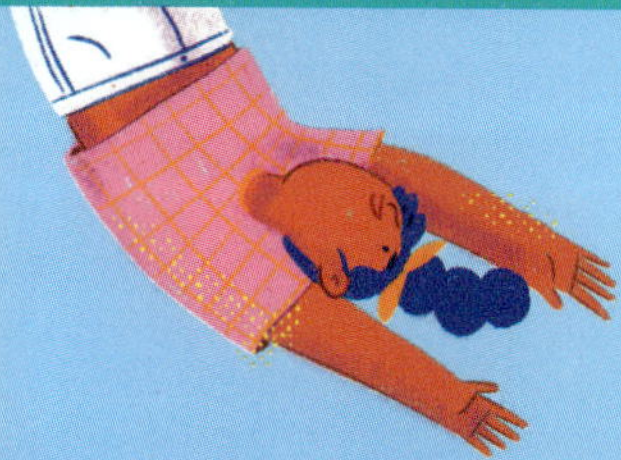

I'm grateful for...

....

....

....

17

Make a photo display of you and your family.

TELL YOUR STORY

to own it

Your story is unique and you are the one who gets to tell it.

Celebrate your story and feel proud of who you are!

What are you proud of?

Who gave you your name? Does it have a meaning?

What is your favorite thing to do with your family?

What do you want your life to be like when you grow up?

Do you know any stories about your family?

My Story

Ask your family to help you find photos of yourself as a baby and growing up. Make frames and stick the pictures in them. Here are some ideas...

Baby Me

School Me

Cool Me

Your family is part of your story. Families are all different - they don't always look how you'd expect. Make a family tree like this one.

Who do you live with?

What other children are in your family?

Who is oldest in your family?

Who is youngest?

Who in your family lives close by?

Who in your family lives far away?

Draw your tree onto a large piece of cardstock or paper. Stick the photos on or draw your family... or get them to draw themselves!

18

Make paper airplanes to fly your fears away.

FACE YOUR FEARS

to see that you are stronger than them

Fears tell us so much. Which ones can we work through and let go of?

The mouse looks huge – that's really scary!

Sometimes we get scared, even when we're not in danger.

But look – now we can see the mouse is small and cute.

Make paper airplanes to fly your fears away

1 Find a rectangular piece of paper and write your fears and worries on it.

2 Fold the paper in half lengthways.

3 Open it out again and fold two corners in to meet in the middle.

4 Fold the edges again to meet in the middle.

5 Fold your airplane in half so that the flaps are on the outside.

Something new or different can feel scary, even if it's not dangerous. It takes strength to let your fears go.

Make paper airplanes to help you.

6 Fold the edges down like this.

7 Now you're ready to let your fears fly away.

Once you've finished folding your paper airplane, launch it, and watch your fears fly away!

19

Make and twirl a fidget spinner.

KEEP YOUR COOL

to handle those big emotions

Learning how to calm your feelings takes practice. Big emotions are like clouds – they pass across the sky. You can watch them go. They don't stick around very long.

Sadness might feel like a gray, rainy day.

Fear can make you freeze like snow.

But feelings pass. Before you know it, you'll feel sunny again.

Anger can feel like a storm inside you.

Moving your body can help stormy emotions feel calm again. Try these things.

Make a calming fidget spinner

1. Cut out circles from thin cardstock. Copy the patterns below or design your own.
2. Push a coin through the center and spin to see the calming patterns.

20
Write an imaginative puppy adventure story.

FIND TIME TO BE ALONE

– you'll be in good company

When you feel good hanging out with yourself, you can create happiness anywhere, anytime.

Have fun exploring your limitless imagination.

Think of stories or poems to write. Maybe you like to make music, or invent new dances. Keep a book of your ideas.

When you're by yourself, you can go at your own pace. What will you find?

Magical things happen when you spend time alone. What will you discover?

Write a story about Patch the dog. Draw pictures to go with your story. Here are some ideas...

21

See life from a different point of view.

CHOOSE ANOTHER STORY

to see a different point of view

There is often more than one way to see things. Look carefully.

What do you see? Turn the book upside down to see the answer.

Do you see rabbits or ducks?
They are both there.

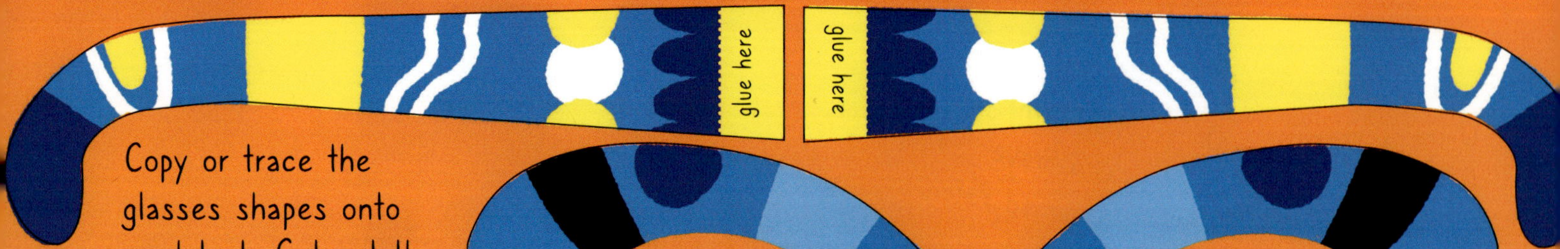

Copy or trace the glasses shapes onto cardstock. Cut out the glasses. Fold along the dotted lines and glue the arms to the back of the frames.

There's always more than one way to look at things.
Try to find a positive story.

A long journey can be boring...

...or the chance to imagine a perfect adventure!

Put on the glasses when you need to remind yourself to look at things in a different way.

What do you see?

22

Save your sunflower seeds to make seedy, cheesy bread sticks.

BUILD PATIENCE

– it's worth the wait

Plant a tiny sunflower seed in the ground. Be patient.

When you feel OK about waiting, life gets a lot less frustrating. Practice being patient by growing a sunflower.

After 16 weeks, you can collect the seeds to eat!

Bake seedy, cheesy breadsticks

Ingredients

- 3/4 cup bread flour
- 1/8 cup cheddar cheese
- 100ml warm water
- 1 tsp salt
- 1 tsp oil
- 1 tbsp sunflower seeds
- 1 tsp yeast

Equipment

- bowl
- cheese grater
- tea towel
- baking tray
- wooden spoon
- baking paper
- patience!

1 Put all the ingredients into a bowl. Mix everything together until you have a ball of dough.

2 Cover the bowl with a damp tea towel. Leave in a warm place for an hour. Wait patiently.

There are all sorts of ways to practice being patient.

When it's raining outside...

...build a domino run inside.

When it's dry outdoors...

...collect and arrange colored leaves in a pattern.

3 After one hour, remove the tea towel. How much has your dough risen?

4 Tear the dough into six pieces. Roll and squash them into sausage shapes.

5 Put your seedy breadsticks onto a baking tray.

6 Ask an adult to help you bake them for 20 minutes or until golden brown.

Enjoy your seedy, cheesy breadsticks. They were worth the wait!

23

Create and decorate an amazing mask.

IMAGINE

to explore your creativity

When you use your imagination, anything is possible.

Copy or trace the mask onto cardstock. Use your imagination to decorate it.

Welcome to the masquerade ball!
What will you dress up as?

Cut out your mask and secure it with some ribbon tied to the sides or a straw glued to one side to hold it with.

24

Draw little pictures to go on a scavenger hunt.

SPEND TIME IN NATURE

to find your happy place

Being outdoors is good for you in so many ways. All your senses work to make you feel happier. Step outside and explore your garden, park, or nearby woodland.

What can you smell?

What can you hear?

What can you see?

Go barefoot to let the grass tickle your feet.

Get closer to nature

Climb a tree.

Make bark rubbings.

Build a den.

Go on a nature scavenger hunt

Draw pictures like the ones along the bottom of the pages and cut them out. Take them with you outdoors.

When you spot something, put the picture in a jar. What did you see?

25

Share a colorful heart to feel close.

EASE INTO CHANGE

– things can work out

When things change, it can feel scary and exciting at the same time.

A butterfly changes many times in its lifespan.

Some changes can be really hard. When you miss someone, talking about your feelings helps your heart feel happier.

Copy these hearts onto cardstock and cut them out. When you're away from someone special, give them one half and keep the other, so you can still feel close.

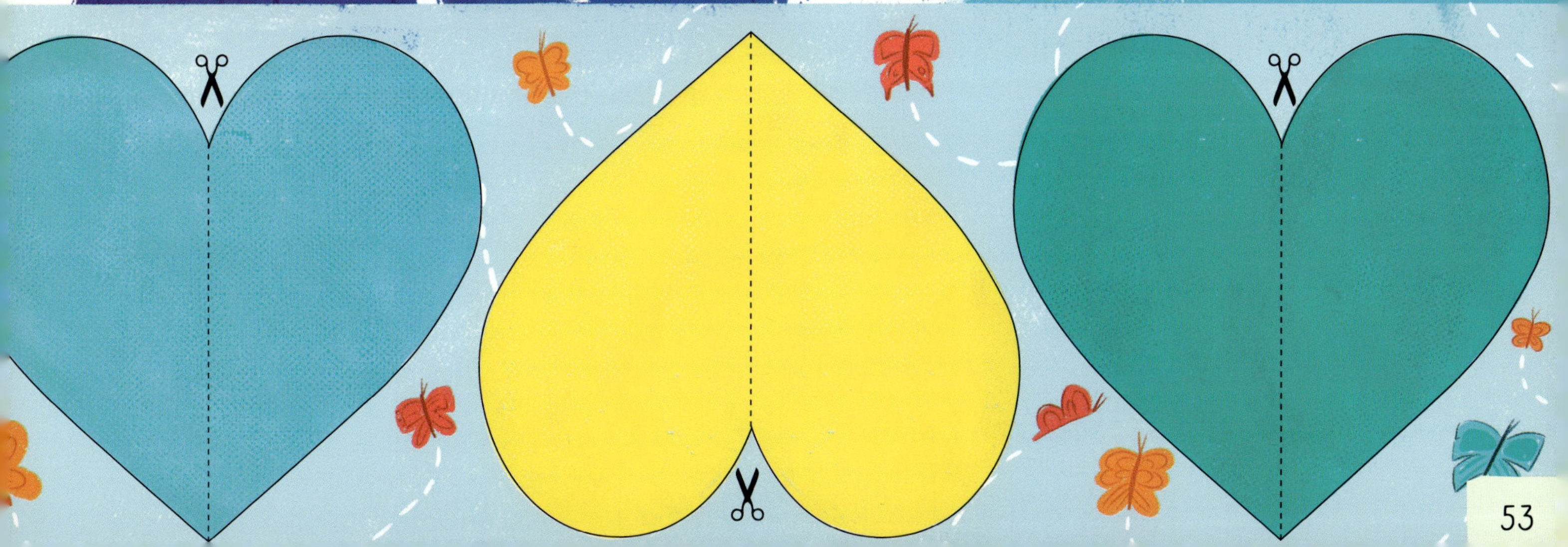

26

Create your own mini film set.

CREATE

to set your imagination free

When you create something unique, your mind feels happy, calm, and free. Use pens and pencils to draw a fantastic place from your imagination.

What adventures could happen?

What would happen if the characters below visited your imagined place?

Create your own miniature film set in a shoebox. Use recycled and craft materials to decorate the box and to make furniture, props, and sets.

What kind of building will you create?

Copy the characters shown below onto cardstock and cut them out. Fold back the tabs. Choose your cast.

Now you're ready to direct your first film!

27

Meet up to play dragons and ladders.

GET TOGETHER

to share happiness

Being around other people - especially the ones who love and accept you - builds happiness. Who makes you feel happy?

Use cardstock to make a spinner and some counters like the ones shown here. Stick a pencil through the hole in the spinner, pointy end down.

How to play dragons and ladders

1 Choose a counter each. Decide who will go first.

2 Spin the spinner and move your counter the number of steps the spinner lands on.

3 If you land on a ladder, climb up it.

4 If you land on a dragon, slide down it.

5 The winner is the first to reach the 100 square.

28

Post a hug to someone you can't see.

HUG

to hold each other close

A hug helps calm your emotions and makes you feel good.

Try a handshake, fist bump, elbow tap, wave, or wink, too!

If there is someone you can't hug in person, send a paper hug.

Being close to a tree makes you feel calm. Find a tree and hug it close.

The tree is alive, like you. Can you feel it growing?

Draw some hugs onto cardstock and cut out. Write a lovely message to someone special. Use snail mail to send your hug.

29

Make a window picture for your neighbors.

BE GENEROUS

to spread happiness

You are special and your kindness can make the world a brighter place.

Paint a picture or message on a pebble and leave it to be found.

Hide pebbles with happy words and pictures on them in your park or on your walk to school. Make someone smile today!

Passersby will love seeing your picture lit up.

Make a window picture

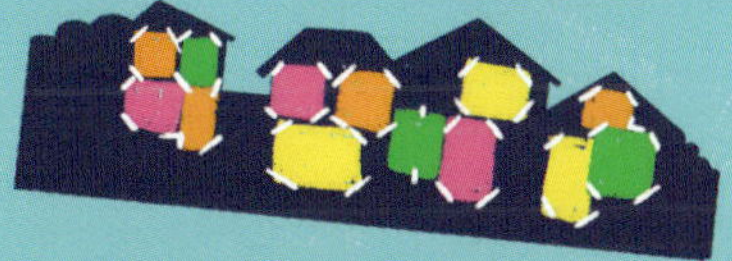

1 Make up a window picture onto thin cardstock. Carefully cut out the row of houses and cut out their windows.

2 Stick strips of colorful tissue paper over the windows.

3 Hang your masterpiece in your window.

30

Play a guessing game to explore different feelings.

SHOW UNDERSTANDING

by imagining how others feel

When it is hard to understand people and what they do, try to see life from their view. Imagine you could live their life and walk in their shoes.

Play feelings charades

All you need is some friends and a scarf.

HAPPY

ANGRY

WORRIED

PROUD

Showing you care can be enough to make someone feel better.

When someone's feeling down, kind words are like a big umbrella on a rainy day.

EXCITED

SURPRISED

SAD

AFRAID

How to play

1. Cut out small squares of cardstock and write a feelings word on each card. Shuffle them.
2. Pick a card each. Without looking at the card, put it on your forehead, facing out, with a scarf holding it in place.
3. Take turns to ask questions to help you guess your card, but be careful not to name any feelings in your questions.
4. Keep going until everyone has correctly guessed their card.

Published in 2026 by Windmill Books,
an Imprint of Rosen Publishing
2544 Clinton St.
Buffalo, NY 14224

Written by Poppy O'Neill
Illustrated by Caribay M. Benavides
Consultant: Wynne Kinder, MEd
Designer: Lee-May Lim
Additional design: Becca Wildman
Editor: Penny Arlon
Additional Editors:Toni Stemp and Honor Head
Art Director: Stuart Smith

Cataloging-in-Publication Data
Names: O'Neill, Poppy, author. | Benavides, Caribay M., illustrator.
Title: The book that makes you feel happy / by Poppy O'Neill, illustrated by Caribay M. Benavides.
Description: Buffalo, NY : Windmill Books, 2026. | Series: The extraordinary activity library
Identifiers: ISBN 9781725396739 (pbk.) | ISBN 9781725396746 (library bound) | ISBN 9781725396753 (ebook)
Subjects: LCSH:Happiness--Juvenile literature. | Mindfulness--Juvenile literature. |
Self-actualization (Psychology)--Juvenile literature.
Classification: LCC BF575.H27 O64 2026 | DDC 158.1'3--dc23

Printed in the United States of America

CPSIA Compliance Information: Batch #CSWM26
For Further Information contact Rosen Publishing at 1-800-237-9932

Find us on